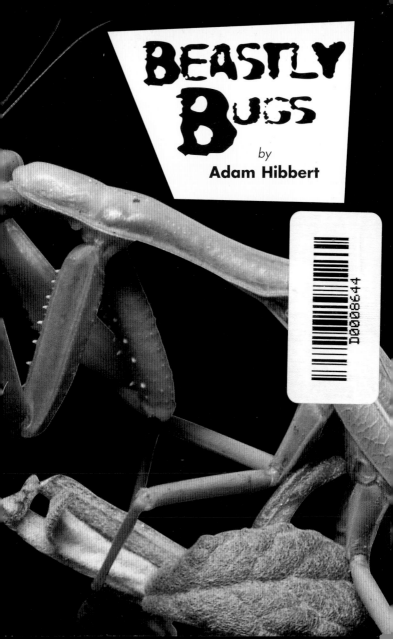

BEASTLY BUGS

by

Adam Hibbert

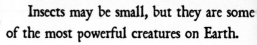

MIGHTY BUGS

Insects may be small, but they are some of the most powerful creatures on Earth. Relative to their size, bugs are record-breakers in weight lifting, jumping, sprinting, and other physical feats.

BRAIN BONUS

What insect can run the fastest?

a) American cockroach
b) goliath beetle
c) African tiger beetle

What is the world's loudest insect?

a) honeybee
b) African cicada
c) cricket

If you could jump as high as a flea, how high could you jump?

a) onto an elephant's back
b) over the U.S. Capitol building
c) over Mount Everest

(answers on page 32)

BEEFY BEETLES

The scarab beetle family reigns supreme in the beetle kingdom. It includes the heaviest beetle in the world, the goliath beetle (which weighs 3.5 ounces—almost as much as a quarter-pound cheeseburger!), and the strongest weight lifter, the rhinoceros beetle. A third scarab record-breaker is the dung beetle, which can move balls of manure hundreds of times heavier than its own weight.

Three-horned rhino beetle

SUPER-BEETLE

The rhinoceros beetle can hold 850 times its own weight. If you were that strong, you could lift ten elephants!

Cat flea

SO LONG, SUCKER!

Fleas, like this cat flea, are the world's most amazing jumpers. At an average .05 inch long, fleas can jump as far as 13 inches, or 220 times their own length. If you could jump so well, you would be able to jump a quarter of a mile in one hop!

ROACH RUNNER

Cockroaches may look clunky and heavy, but don't be fooled; they are actually very fit. Scientists have figured out that at least one kind of cockroach can run at 3.4 mph, covering a distance 50 times its own body length every second. If you could do that, you'd be sprinting at 200 mph!

IN A FLAP

Some insects are record-breakers whether or not you allow for their size. The fastest muscles in the world belong to the tiny midge fly, which beats its wings 62,760 times a minute (or 1,046 times a second)—much too fast to see with the naked eye.

EENSY WEENSY

Spiders are among the world's most successful predators—
they eat more animals than all the lions, tigers,
sharks, and grizzly bears combined. Spiders
actually aren't insects but arachnids. Unlike insects,
which have six legs, arachnids have eight legs. Almost
all spiders have venomous fangs, and some
use their silken threads to make traps.

Raft spider

RAFT RAIDER

Very few spiders live
underwater, but some
catch fish! The raft spider
spreads its legs out over the surface of a pond to
feel the vibrations of passing prey. When a little
fish or tadpole comes in range, the raft spider
plunges into the water, grabs its victim,
and takes it back onto dry land to eat.

Tarantula

HAIRY HUNTER

Tarantulas are well known for their big
bodies and hairy legs. Almost all of them
hunt at night, sometimes catching insects, mice, and even
snakes. In South America, some orb weaver spiders spin
webs big enough to catch small birds and bats.

A hungry tarantula is a serious threat to small snakes. The spider's venom quickly subdues the snake—now the spider is ready for the kill!

THE POISONER POISONED!

STUCK ON YOU

For some spiders, spinning sticky threads is less important than being able to spit. Spitting spiders have developed a special glue that they make in the glands other spiders use for venom. When they see prey or an enemy, they spit the glue at it, sticking it to the spot!

DINNER DATE

Spiders are incredibly skillful at catching insects. The bolas spiders of the Americas, Africa, and Australia hang from a twig and dangle a silken thread with a sticky glue tip. The sticky tip mimics the scent of a female moth, luring male moths within striking distance.

BRAIN BONUS

What do the Trobriand Islanders use the webs of the giant wood spider for?

a) fishing nets
b) silk underwear
c) shopping baskets

How many different kinds of silk does a garden spider make?

a) 2–3
b) 4–5
c) 7–8

Which of these spiders builds its nest underground?

a) a tarantula
b) a brown recluse
c) a trap-door spider

(answers on page 32)

5

I MARRIED A CANNIBAL!

BRAIN BONUS

Why do some people call the praying mantid "mule killer"?

a) Very hungry mantids eat mules.
b) Mantids scare mules to death.
c) If a mule ate a mantid, it would die.

How does a male orb weaver spider tell a female not to eat him when he steps onto her web?

a) He plucks the web like a guitar.
b) He whistles.
c) He carries a pink rose.

Why does one type of firefly imitate the mating signals of another firefly species?

a) to tease them
b) to make her mates jealous
c) to lure and capture the male

(answers on page 32)

MATE ESCAPE

The male king baboon spider has special hooks on his legs that hold the female's fangs during mating.

The black widow spider got its name from the female's notorious habit of eating the male after mating, leaving herself a widow. This doesn't always happen, however. If the female is well fed, the male can escape and mate again.

Jumping spider

WHAT'S FOR DINNER, MOM?

Female spiders aren't always the ones eating dinner; sometimes they *are* dinner. The female of some species of the *coelotes* spider will die in her web, allowing her young to feed on her body.

MUNCHED MANTID

The female praying mantid may be the most dangerous mate in the world. Like the black widow spider, the female mantid sometimes feasts on her partner after mating. The male is adapted to cope with the danger of being eaten before completing the task, and his body will continue to mate with a female even after she has bitten his head off.

MY MATE, MY DINNER

Male bugs often provide dinner for their mate: unfortunately
for the males, they're the main course! By eating their mates,
females benefit from having a handy snack just as their eggs
are growing. Males also benefit in a way, by making it more
likely that their offspring will have a healthy mother.

PRAYING OR PREYING?

The praying mantid, or mantis, takes its name from
the special way in which it holds its forelegs in front of its
head; in this position, it look as if it is praying. This creature
is a ferocious carnivore from the very start: newly
hatched mantids often eat each other.

Praying mantid

STRENGTH IN NUMBERS

On their own, some insects wouldn't last long, but when they join forces they can achieve amazing things. Ants, as well as bees and termites, live together in colonies that can number in the thousands.

Each member of the colony has a specific job, from caring for the young to gathering food to defending the nest from enemies.

Bulldog ant

BULLDOG BITES!

Because they are born to do different jobs, ants in the same nest can be all sorts of different shapes and sizes. The longest worker ants in the world are the bulldog ants of Australia, which can be up to 1.5 inches long. They come equipped with powerful spiked jaws, or mandibles, and a stinger that can potentially kill people.

If you were as strong as an ant, you could carry a blue whale calf weighing 3 tons!

AWESOME ANT-MAN

HOSTILE TAKEOVERS

Some species of ants attack the nests of other species, stealing young ants and bringing them up as workers. One type of ant queen in Africa lets enemy ants drag her into their nest, where she kills their queen and takes over!

ON THE MARCH

Army ants form columns up to 330 feet long and 3 feet wide, marching around South America, eating everything in their path. Some villages make army ants welcome, moving their farm animals out of the way so that the ants can gobble up all the village's mice and other vermin.

Ant army

SEW CUTE

Some ants use their larvae, or newly hatched ants, for building nests. The weaver ant larva produces silk in a long strand. The adult weaver ants then use their larvae as needles and thread, poking them through the edges of leaves to stitch them together, making a cozy nest.

BRAIN BONUS

Why is the silver ant of the Sahara Desert happy when the temperature hits 120 °F?

a) It likes to sunbathe.
b) It eats the frazzled insects.
c) It's a good excuse for a siesta.

How many aphids can a large red ant colony eat in a day?

a) 1,000
b) 100,000
c) 1,000,000

African termites can build nests as high as...

a) 6 feet
b) 27 feet
c) 42 feet

(answers on page 32)

NOW YOU SEE IT, NOW YOU DON'T

Insects make a tasty snack for birds, lizards, snakes, and small mammals. Some rely on a quick getaway, but many are masters of disguise, blending in with their surroundings to escape notice.

HUGE HERCULES

No amount of disguise can hide the Hercules emperor moth. Its wings are 10 inches wide— as big as a dinner plate!

INVISIBLE VANDALS

The buffalo treehopper looks exactly like a leaf. Less than an inch long, it can cause serious damage in orchards, particularly to young apple trees. Females cut slits into the tree bark and lay their eggs inside. These slits let fungi and diseases into the branches.

Buffalo treehopper

MOTH FASHION

In Britain, peppered moths that were light gray were once more numerous than dark gray ones—they blended in better with the tree bark and were thus less likely to be eaten by birds. But in the middle of the 19th century, soot from the new factories blackened the trees, and the dark gray moths now blended in better—and the number of light gray moths declined.

FIERCE FLOWER

Although all praying mantids are good at hiding among leaves, the flower mantid is champion. With its bright pink coat and knobbly growths over its body, the flower mantid remains hidden inside a flower, or it can impersonate a flower on its own. Insects arriving at the "flower" for a snack are in for a deadly surprise!

Stick insect

WALKING STICKS

Stick insects are so good at pretending to be twigs on a plant that birds are more likely to try to perch on them than eat them. Unlike many camouflaged bugs, which have to stay completely still to blend into the background, stick insects bend their knees rhythmically, pretending to sway in the breeze.

BRAIN BONUS

How did the phantom midge get its name?

a) Its larvae are transparent.
b) It appears only at night.
c) It makes a wailing noise.

Which insect builds its home from anything it can find?

a) a bag-lady moth
b) a caddis fly larva
c) a bumblebee

Which insect can change color to match its surroundings?

a) a stick insect
b) a chameleon ant
c) a blushing butterfly

(answers on page 32)

THIS SUCKS!

There are at least 750 different species of leech in the world, from pond dwellers to land lurkers. Some of them are the world's most specialized bloodsuckers, and their peculiar talents have even earned them a role in medicine.

BRAIN BONUS

How does a leech breathe?

a) It sucks oxygenated blood from animals.
b) through its skin
c) through its nose

How do aquatic leeches get into their victims' nostrils?

a) They hide in handkerchiefs.
b) via drinking water
c) They lurk under fingernails.

What's a seagoing marine leech's favorite place for a meal?

a) a penguin's beak
b) the gills of a fish
c) the eyeball of an octopus

(answers on page 32)

DOCTOR LEECH

Leeches were a popular tool for early medical practitioners. (The word *leech* comes from the Old English word for "doctor.") Doctors believed that some illnesses were caused by high blood pressure and used leeches to drain blood from their patients. The patients often decided that they suddenly felt much better, rather than go through the treatment again!

Medicinal leech

LONG-LIVED LEECH

Leeches have been known to live for up to 27 years— that's longer than a tiger!

NOSEBLEED

Some unlucky birds and cattle are killed by leeches, but not because they lose too much blood. In very rare incidents, a leech may climb inside its victim's nostrils to suck blood. As the leech swells with blood, the nose can be blocked and the animal suffocates.

LEECH LUNCH

Not all species of leech are bloodsuckers. They can be accomplished swimmers and crawlers, hunting down and eating slow-moving prey, such as snails, worms, and insect larvae. Their eggs are laid in a cocoon of slime and hatch into fully formed miniature leeches.

DRIPPING BLOOD

The bloodsucking leeches of the world have three jaws that make a Y-shaped cut in your skin. Their saliva is specially developed to stop your blood from clotting. You may not notice a leech bite until the leech, fat with your blood, has left, leaving behind a cut that won't stop bleeding.

HUNGRY HERBIVORES

Insects aren't just troublesome because they bite us. Swarms of them can also be a serious danger to plant life, threatening starvation for plant-eating creatures. Even in high-tech countries, farmers can have their businesses ruined by bug armies.

FLYING PIG

Polyphemus moth caterpillars eat 86,000 times their weight in two months. If a human baby ate that much, it would feast on 36 elephants!

Cabbage white caterpillar

SLOW SLURPER

Even the seemingly harmless slug can cause serious crop damage. Using its rasping tongue, a slug can chomp through important crops, such as potatoes, wheat, carrots, and green vegetables.

BRAIN BONUS

One swarm of locusts in North America in 1872 covered an area as big as...

a) 12 square miles
b) 1,240 square miles
c) 3,224 square miles

How tall can a desert locust swarm become?

a) quarter of a mile
b) half a mile
c) 1 mile

Gardeners use bowls of _____ to catch slugs.

a) yogurt
b) beer
c) milk

(answers on page 32)

STOMACHS WITH WINGS!

Locust

Locusts can be deadly pests, massing in huge swarms. The desert locust of Africa and the Middle East moves in swarms of up to a billion, eating in one day as much as half a million people eat in one year. Locust swarms cause car accidents by covering roads in a squishy, slippery coating of squashed locust bodies!

CABBAGE CARNAGE

The caterpillar of the European cabbage butterfly loves to munch on cabbages, making it very unpopular with cabbage farmers. Once unknown in the Americas, the butterfly was accidentally transported to North America in the 1860s, where it caused heavy losses in the cabbage crop.

HAIR THEY ARE

Even if you don't have a single dust mite in your home, you probably have other mites living in your skin. Follicle mites, about .01 inch long, like nothing better than the cozy little gap around the roots of hairs, and they are especially fond of eyelashes. Scientists aren't sure what they eat there, but they are believed to be harmless.

BRAIN BONUS

Although this insect eats bedbugs, why wouldn't you want a masked bedbug hunter in your bed?

a) Hunting in a mask is bad manners.
b) It bites humans, too.
c) It stays up late playing loud music.

Does the earwig have anything to do with ears?

a) No, nothing.
b) Yes, it eats ear wax.
c) Not really—it just likes hiding in small spaces!

Why would a bedbug change color from brown to dull red?

a) It has just eaten a meal of blood.
b) It is sunburned.
c) It is blushing.

(answers on page 32)

TINY MITE

Dust mites forage through the fibers of your mattress, cushions, carpet, and anywhere else that flakes of old skin might collect. Their droppings are so tiny that they can float in the air in just the same way as pollen grains, causing some people to have an allergic reaction like hay fever.

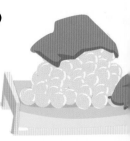

EGGS-AUSTING!

A well-fed female bedbug can lay 600 eggs in your bed every year!

MICRO MONSTERS

You might think that you haven't yet met a beastly bug today, but you certainly have; you just didn't notice it. In every house there are millions of bugs too small to see with the naked eye, from dust mites that feed off flakes of skin trapped in the carpet to dried-up tardigrades waiting for rain.

Prostigmatid mite

BLOWING IN THE WIND

If you're reading this on a dry day, you've probably already breathed in a few tardigrades, or water bears. Less than .04 inch long—much too small to see without a microscope—these moisture-loving minibeasts dry up and blow around in the wind until they find a nice, moist new habitat.

Bedbug

THAT REALLY BUGS ME

The most annoying housemate you are likely to meet is the bedbug, but it's usually up and about long before you are. The bedbug uses its pointy beak to saw through your skin and suck your blood while you're asleep. Don't worry, though—it's so tiny you barely feel it.

SUPER-SLIMY

Snails and slugs are gastropods (the name *gastropod* means "stomach foot"). Most slugs and snails chomp on plants, but some will chew anything—including other snails and slugs! There are some gastropods that live in ponds and rivers and even under the sea. They are also divided into those that have shells and those that don't.

BRAIN BONUS

What's the average speed of a garden snail?

a) .03 mph
b) .3 mph
c) 3 mph

How old is the oldest snail?

a) 5 years
b) 10 years
c) 20 years

The largest snails in the world live under the sea near Australia. How much do they weigh?

a) 2 pounds
b) 22 pounds
c) 40 pounds

(answers on page 32)

CUPID'S ARROWS

Some types of snails and slugs are hermaphrodites, meaning they are both male and female. When two cone snails decide to reproduce, they inject each other with little darts. The darts contain sperm, which find their own way to the unfertilized eggs in each snail.

African giant snail

YELLOW SLUGMARINE

Slugs have glamorous relatives that live in the sea. Sea slugs have gills for breathing underwater and specialize in eating poisonous animals such as jellyfish. They recycle their prey's poison to make themselves poisonous. Sea slugs are very colorful, which in the animal world often means, "I'm poisonous!"

Thick-horned aeolid, a kind of sea slug

BUILD IT YOURSELF

Snails build their own shells to protect themselves from the outside world. As the snail grows bigger, it simply adds on to its shell. Snail shells are usually spiral but can also have knobs, curls, or spines.

A CRACKING CONCERN

Snails are a favorite food of many creatures, including birds, frogs, snakes, skunks—even humans. Some birds crack snails' shells by dropping them on rocks.

GIGANTIC GASTROPOD

The African giant snail is the largest land snail, growing up to 16 inches long, with an 8-inch shell, and weighing up to 2 pounds. Some scientists have suggested that these snails could be farmed as a food for humans. They are very cheap to farm and very meaty!

VENOM MONSTER

Centipedes use the pointed claws at the end of their first pair of legs to inject venom into their prey. You don't have to worry about most centipedes, because their claws aren't strong enough to pierce your skin. But the bright blue Malayan centipede can break the skin and cause months of illness.

What does *Myriapoda* (the Latin name for centipedes and millipedes) mean?

a) many feet
b) beautiful nose
c) shiny shoes

How fast can the fastest centipede run?

a) 2 inches a second
b) 6 inches a second
c) 20 inches a second

Why is one European centipede called Electricus?

a) It eats wiring.
b) It glows in the dark.
c) It is used for manufacturing lightbulbs.

(answers on page 32)

MILD-MANNERED

Millipedes don't have claws, preferring fruit and leaves to meat, but they can be just as poisonous as centipedes. If a millipede is disturbed, it will secrete poison from glands on the sides of its body. Some millipedes produce cyanide that oozes out of their pores.

Giant millipede

750-FOOT CREATURE!

How do you tell millipedes and centipedes apart? Millipedes usually have round bodies (although some are flat), while centipedes are always flat. Also, millipedes have two pairs of legs on each segment of their bodies, and centipedes have only one pair. Although they don't have a million feet, millipedes can have anywhere from 24 to 750 feet!

LOADS OF LEGS

The leggiest members of the crawling world are the
myriapods, otherwise known as centipedes and millipedes.
When you do a lot of rummaging under rotting leaves and
in tiny spaces in the soil, it helps if you're
long and thin and have lots of legs.

Centipede

OLD-TIMER

The centipede wins the award for oldest fossilized land animal.
Found in a rock estimated to be 414 million years old, its tracks have
also been found in rocks dating back to 465 million years ago!

**Millipedes may win a leg competition, but
centipedes would win a length competition—
they can grow longer than a foot!**

LONG vs.
LEGGY

SMALL BUT DEADLY

Rat flea

Some seemingly harmless insects are made deadly by the diseases they can spread. So don't worry about venomous spiders, angry scorpions, or exotic, poisonous centipedes. More of a threat are the tiny mosquito, the humdrum housefly, and the fearsome flea.

FILTHY FEET

Houseflies taste their food— anything from garbage to your dinner—with their feet, leaving behind bacteria and disease when they land on your food.

SWAT SENSATION

Flies can spread such dangerous diseases as cholera, typhoid, leprosy, diphtheria, smallpox, and polio. Killing these insects can help stop the spread of disease. In 1933, the citizens of Tokyo in Japan rallied round for *Haotor*, or "National Fly-Catching Day," and killed 117,500,000 of the little pests.

FLEA FEAR

There are many different kinds of flea, from the rat flea to a giant flea found in the nests of mountain beavers in North America. The most dangerous flea, as far as humans are concerned, is the oriental rat flea, the most effective carrier of bubonic plague, or the Black Death.

PLAGUE PANIC

In the 14th century, over a quarter of the population of Europe was wiped out by the Black Death. In some villages, there were more people dead than alive. Outbreaks of plague continued for centuries. It wasn't until 1894 that doctors finally discovered that bubonic plague is spread by fleas.

MOSQUITO MENACE

If a mosquito's bite left only an itchy sore, it might not be considered such a menace. The mosquito jabs its snout through your skin and then spits saliva into the wound. The saliva is meant to stop the blood from clotting, but it can also contain killer diseases like yellow fever and malaria.

Yellow fever mosquito

BRAIN BONUS

How many people die each year from mosquito-related illnesses?
a) 10,000
b) 100,000
c) over 1,000,000

How many people died in the 14th century from bubonic plague?
a) 2.5 million
b) 25 million
c) 250 million

How long does the average male housefly live?
a) 10 days
b) 20 days
c) 3 months

(answers on page 32)

STING IN THEIR TAIL

The most famous arachnids are probably spiders. But the deadliest, most notorious of the group is the scorpion, with its powerful claws, scuttling legs, and nasty sting at the end of its body.

BRAIN BONUS

How long was the longest live scorpion ever measured?

a) 3.7 inches
b) 7.4 inches
c) 11.4 inches

How big was the biggest prehistoric scorpion, which lived 300 million years ago?

a) 1.3 feet
b) 2.8 feet
c) 4 feet

How long will a dog survive after being stung by the northern African fat-tailed scorpion?

a) 7 hours
b) 24 hours
c) 1 week

(answers on page 32)

DEADLY DANCE

The scorpion male has to be extremely careful when approaching a mate. One type of male grasps the female by the claws and "dances" her around, sometimes for hours. Then it places a parcel of sperm on the ground and pulls the female onto it. Many males fail to get away before they are eaten alive.

POISON PARENTS

Despite their poisonous reputation, scorpions can be some of the most caring mothers in the arachnid world. The female scorpion gives birth to live young rather than laying eggs. She protects them by carrying them around on her back, feeding them until they've grown enough to fend for themselves.

Living on baking-hot rocks, scorpions sometimes stand on tiptoes to cool off.

Scorpion

MEAN MACHINE

The scorpion is also equipped with a powerful pair of pincers, called pedipalps. After the scorpion has paralyzed its prey with poison, it uses the claws to crush and tear apart the meal and to bring snippets of meat to its mouth. Actually, out of 1,500 scorpion species, fewer than 25 are lethal. The nonlethal ones rely on their strong pedipalps to deal with prey.

HEY, BIG STINGER!

The emperor scorpion has a typical stinger. Connected to two poison glands in the body, the needle can be flicked forward over the scorpion's head to kill prey or to defend the scorpion from menaces, such as humans. Worldwide, over 5,000 people die from scorpion stings each year.

Emperor scorpion

BRAIN BONUS

An insect's suit of armor needs regular, careful cleaning, otherwise it...

a) rusts
b) upsets the insect's mother
c) gets attacked by fungus

Beetles are the largest insect group. How many species are there?

a) over 350
b) over 35,000
c) over 350,000

How hot is the jet of chemicals from a bombardier beetle's bottom?

a) 122°F
b) 167°F
c) 212°F

(answers on page 32)

SNAPPY STAG

Sometimes called a pinching bug, the stag beetle is smaller than the rhino beetle, but it has pincers that can draw blood if they clamp hold of your finger. It only attacks if provoked, preferring to forage for sap among rotting wood.

FLAME THROWER

The bombardier beetle uses an amazing "flame-throwing" technique to fend off enemies: it squirts a boiling jet of noxious vapor from its bottom!

Stag b

RHINO RAGE

Despite their fearsome appearance, rhino beetles aren't all that aggressive and can't use their "horns" to hurt humans. The horns are used to show off to females.

If two males are competing for one female, they will use their horns for wrestling, trying to topple their rival onto his back.

ARMOR PLATING

Beetles are the tanks of the insect world. Some have developed thick armor plating, which allows them to fight, hunt dangerous creatures, and avoid being eaten themselves. The hard shells are made of a material called chitin (pronounced KITE-en).

INSIDE OUT

Rhino beetles

Beefier beetles, such as rhinoceros beetles, have very strong armor. As with all insects, this is so tough that they don't need a skeleton; they use their casing as an external skeleton, or "exoskeleton," with muscles and internal organs attached to it from the inside.

DUNG LOVERS

The male minotaur beetle brings a rabbit dropping to its family for the beetle grubs to eat.

FIG FEAST

Despite their name, dung beetles don't eat just poop. Scientists in Borneo recently caught a .2-inch-long dung beetle cutting itself a chunk of fig, which it buried to feed its offspring. This species of dung beetle was thought to be rare until scientists learned to look for it near fig trees.

MOBILE HOME

Dung beetles range in size from .2 inch to 1 inch, gathering and burying animal dung to eat. In this way they act like nature's own muck spreaders, enriching the soil. Some dung beetles are very hard workers, fashioning dung into a ball and rolling it several feet to their burrow.

Dung beetle

WONDER WORM

Another contributor to fertile soil is the common earthworm. On a damp night you can catch worms dragging leaves down into their burrows. By eating leaves and other rotting plants, worms fertilize the soil. By burrowing, the worms also bring water and air into the soil, further enriching it.

RECYCLING BUGS

Insects and other tiny creatures are the biggest and most vital part of the ecosystem (the network of animals and plants that makes life on Earth possible). Insects and worms help to turn dead animal and plant tissue into soil and nutrients, which other organisms can use to grow.

MIDNIGHT SNACK?

Even though a mole is full, if it spies a tasty earthworm, it will bite the worm's head off and leave it in a "cupboard." The worm doesn't die, but it can't escape without a head. However, if the mole doesn't come back quickly enough, the worm will grow a new head and slink away.

BRAIN BONUS

How many of the Earth's 1,200,000 species so far identified are insects?

a) 50,000
b) 500,000
c) 1,000,000

In which of these places would you be most likely to find an Australian dung beetle?

a) a Sydney sewer
b) a wallaby's bottom
c) a bathroom

How long can a giant earthworm grow?

a) 2.2 feet
b) 3.3 feet
c) 22 feet

(answers on page 32)

SMELLY BUGS

Shield bug

If you're an insect without an armor-thick shell, you could always try putting off predators with a nasty odor. This smelly habit usually works, but not always: the gray meerkat likes to munch stinky millipedes. No one knows why—even the meerkat looks disgusted while it chews!

BIG NOSE

The female emperor moth may be the smelliest insect in the world. In 1961, scientists discovered that the male moths can smell them from up to 7 miles away. The males have very sensitive "noses"—their antennae can detect a single molecule of the female's scent.

BRAIN BONUS

The African milkweed butterfly's scent is actually made up of how many different chemicals?

a) 21
b) 124
c) 214

What is the name of the shield bug that feasts on Colorado beetle grubs?

a) *Podisus*
b) *Spudicus*
c) *Stinkitus*

What shape are an emperor moth's feelers?

a) nose-shaped
b) feather-shaped
c) balloon-shaped

(answers on page 32)

STINKY SHIELD

Some leaf-dwelling bugs look a little like the shields medieval knights used to carry, so they are called shield bugs. But because they are horribly smelly, they are also called stink bugs. Some kinds can grow up to 2 inches long, and one can spit a stinky substance as far as a foot!

ODOR CONTROL

Beetle larvae

Some shield bugs are real pests for farmers. Because they are so stinky, most birds won't eat them, which means they can suck the sap from a cabbage all day without being eaten. But others are helpful: one type likes to munch on the larvae of the Colorado beetle, a major potato pest.

STINK-WICH!

Interested in something more smelly than old cheese? Some people love to eat stink bugs!

BRAIN BONUS ANSWERS

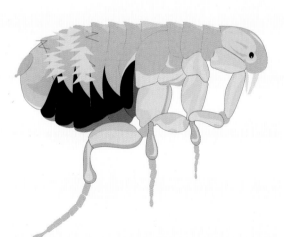

p. 2   **c)** African tiger beetle. It can run 5.6 mph. **b)** African cicada. It is as loud as a jackhammer. **b)** over the U.S. Capitol building.

p. 5   **a)** fishing nets. **c)** 7–8. **c)** a trap-door spider.

p. 6   **c)** If a mule ate a mantid, it would die. **a)** He plucks the web like a guitar. **c)** to lure and capture the male.

p. 9   **b)** It eats the frazzled insects. **b)** 100,000. **c)** 42 feet.

p. 11   **a)** Its larvae are transparent. **b)** a caddis fly larva. a) a stick insect.

p. 12   **b)** through its skin. **b)** via drinking water. **b)** the gills of a fish.

p. 15   **c)** 3,224 sqare miles. **c)** 1 mile. **b)** beer.

p. 16   **b)** It bites humans, too. **c)** Not really—it just likes hiding in small spaces! **a)** It has just eaten a meal of blood.

p. 18   **a)** .03 mph. **c)** 20 years. **c)** 40 pounds.

p. 20   **a)** many feet. **c)** 20 inches a second. **b)** It glows in the dark.

p. 23   **c)** over 1,000,000. **b)** 25 million. **b)** 20 days.

p. 24   **c)** 11.4 inches. **b)** 2.8 feet. **a)** 7 hours.

p. 26   **c)** gets attacked by fungus. **c)** over 350,000. **c)** 212°F.

p. 29   **c)** 1,000,000. **b)** a wallaby's bottom. **c)** 22 feet.

p. 30   **c)** 214. **a)** *Podisus*. **b)** feather-shaped.